Who Was
Ben Franklin?

Who Was
Ben Franklin?

by Dennis Brindell Fradin

illustrated by John O'Brien

Penguin Workshop
An Imprint of Penguin Random House

For two of my biggest fans—my father,
Myron Fradin, and my father-in-law,
Harold Bloom—DBF

For Tess—JOB

PENGUIN WORKSHOP
Penguin Young Readers Group
An Imprint of Penguin Random House LLC

If you purchased this book without a cover, you should be aware that this book is stolen
property. It was reported as "unsold and destroyed" to the publisher, and neither the author
nor the publisher has received any payment for this "stripped book."

Penguin supports copyright. Copyright fuels creativity, encourages diverse voices, promotes
free speech, and creates a vibrant culture. Thank you for buying an authorized edition of this
book and for complying with copyright laws by not reproducing, scanning, or distributing
any part of it in any form without permission. You are supporting writers and allowing
Penguin to continue to publish books for every reader.

The publisher does not have any control over and does not assume any responsibility for
author or third-party websites or their content.

Text copyright © 2002 by Dennis Brindell Fradin. Illustrations copyright © 2002
by John O'Brien. Cover illustration copyright © 2002 by Penguin Random House LLC.
All rights reserved. Published by Penguin Workshop, an imprint of
Penguin Random House LLC, 345 Hudson Street, New York, New York 10014.
PENGUIN and PENGUIN WORKSHOP are trademarks of Penguin Books Ltd.
WHO HQ & Design is a registered trademark of Penguin Random House LLC.
Printed in the USA.

Library of Congress Control Number: 2002280612

ISBN 9780448424958   60 59 58 57 56 55 54 53

Contents

Who Was
Ben Franklin?

Benjamin Franklin was a man of many talents.

He was a statesman. Perhaps only George Washington did more than Ben Franklin did to free the United States from England.

He was a scientist. For one thing, Ben discovered the nature of lightning.

He was an inventor. Thanks to him, we have lightning rods and bifocal glasses.

He was an author. He wrote a famous book about his experiences. And

people still use the phrase "Haste makes waste," and other sayings that Ben made popular.

Ben did much more in his long life. He began America's first general hospital. He started one of America's first libraries. He helped create the United States Postal Service.

Ben did so much that some people claimed he had magical powers. But he was a flesh-and-blood person. In fact, his life was often sad. As a youth he ran away from home because he was beaten. Later, he lived far away from his wife. And a fight over politics came between Ben and his son.

This is the true story of Ben Franklin—statesman, scientist, inventor, author, and human being.

Chapter 1
Catching Lightning a Bottle

On a June day in 1752, a storm approached Philadelphia. The sky grew dark. As thunder rattled the windows, people ran inside. But in a house at the corner of Race and Second streets, two people were getting ready to go *outside*. One was forty-six-year-old Benjamin Franklin. The other was Ben's twenty-one-year-old son William.

SILK KITE

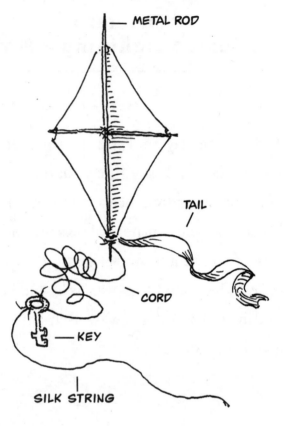

METAL ROD

TAIL

CORD

KEY

SILK STRING

Billy picked up a strange-looking kite. His father had made it for just such a stormy day as this. A metal wire stuck out of the top of the kite. A metal house key was tied to the end of the kite string. Ben grabbed a jar and put it under his coat. The pair dashed through the rain with the kite and the bottle. They stopped when they came to a field.

Billy ran across the field three times trying to fly the kite. Finally, the wind did its work.

Up soared the kite, higher and higher. Soon it was just a speck in the clouds. Ben took the kite string from his son. Then they went into a nearby shed and waited.

As Ben held the kite string, they both felt excited—and scared. With his son's help, Ben was trying to answer an old question. Were lightning and electricity the same thing? Ben suspected that they were. He hoped that flying the kite in the storm would prove it.

Ben believed that electricity in thunderclouds could cause lightning.

The wire on their kite would draw electricity from a cloud, Benjamin hoped. The electricity would run down the kite string to the key. There it would make a spark that he would feel. But the experiment was dangerous. What if a giant lightning bolt struck the kite? The current might kill Ben—and perhaps Billy as well.

As the lightning flashed nearer, Benjamin touched the key. He felt no electric spark. He tried again. Still he felt nothing. Finally, the storm seemed to be overhead. Ben and Billy held their breath as a black cloud swallowed the kite. Benjamin pressed the key. Nothing. Then

suddenly he felt a tingle. He had felt shocks like this before in his lab. A spark from the cloud had electrified the kite. The spark had zoomed down the wet string into the metal key, where Ben could feel it. With Billy's help, he had proved that lightning was electricity!

But the father and son weren't done. Ben took the bottle from beneath his coat.

LEYDEN JAR

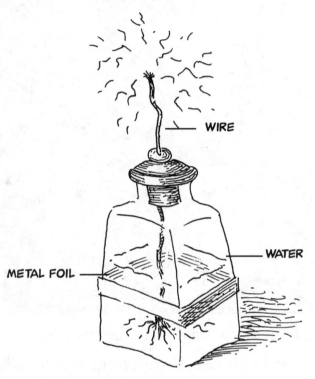

WIRE

WATER

METAL FOIL

It was called a Leyden jar, and it stored electricity. The glass jar had a metal rod sticking out of it. Ben touched the rod of the Leyden jar with the key. The electricity flowed from the key into the bottle. When he finished putting the electricity into the jar, he reeled in the kite. Then Ben and his son went home with the kite and the bottle of electricity.

News of the experiment spread. Ben Franklin became famous for proving that lightning was electricity. But he wasn't satisfied. Now he wanted to make lightning less dangerous. Within a short time, he invented the lightning rod. A metal rod was fixed to the top of a building. When any lightning hit the rod, it would run into the ground through a wire. The building—and the people inside—would not be harmed.

Ben placed a lightning rod on his house. By the end of 1752, other Philadelphia buildings—including the state capitol—also had them. Lightning rods were later put up around the world.

The kite experiment made Ben a famous scientist. His lightning rod made him a famous inventor. He was showered with medals and awards. Because Ben had made lightning less of a danger, some people called him a magician or wizard.

People who knew him laughed at such talk. To them he was the same Ben Franklin they had always known. He was brilliant, to be sure. But he was definitely a man and not a wizard.

Chapter 2
Young Ben

Benjamin Franklin was born in a house on Milk Street in Boston, Massachusetts, on January 17, 1706. There wasn't any United States yet. Massachusetts belonged to England. It was one of England's thirteen American Colonies.

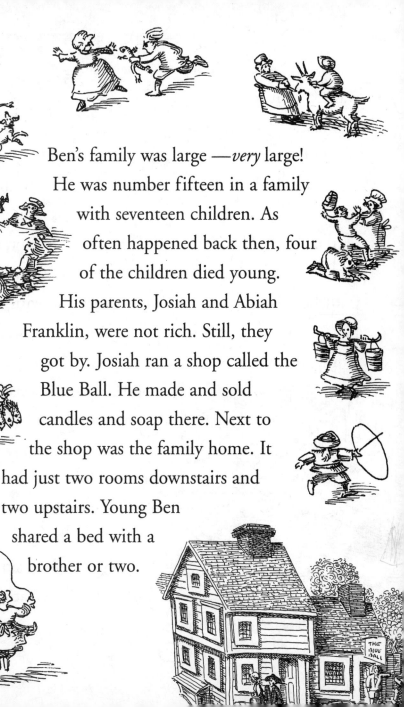

Ben's family was large —*very* large!
He was number fifteen in a family
with seventeen children. As
often happened back then, four
of the children died young.
His parents, Josiah and Abiah
Franklin, were not rich. Still, they
got by. Josiah ran a shop called the
Blue Ball. He made and sold
candles and soap there. Next to
the shop was the family home. It
had just two rooms downstairs and
two upstairs. Young Ben
shared a bed with a
brother or two.

Josiah and Abiah wanted Ben to become a minister. But Ben had two strikes against him. First, he had been born on a Sunday. Many people believed that a Sunday baby was a child of the devil. Also, he was left-handed. That was said to be another mark of the devil. His father punished Ben when he caught him throwing a ball or writing with his left hand. It didn't work. Ben was a lefty for life.

Something else made his parents doubt that Ben would make a good minister. He was a smart aleck. For example, every evening Josiah said a long prayer before supper. One day Ben's father was packing fish into a barrel. Why didn't his father say grace over all the fish in the barrel at once? Ben suggested. Then Josiah would

not have to waste time saying grace at each evening meal! For his smart remark, Ben received a slap.

Ben went to school for just two years, starting at age eight. He failed arithmetic but did well at handwriting and reading. Ben loved books. He read the few books that his family owned. Then he borrowed books from his neighbors. Often he sat up reading most of the night.

He also loved the outdoors. Swimming and kite-flying were his favorite sports. Ben's first invention was for swimmers. He made four

paddles that slipped over his hands and feet. The paddles helped him swim faster.

Ben always looked for new ways to do things. One windy day he was flying a kite

with a friend. They came to a pond. Ben had an idea. He took off his clothes and gave them to his friend. Then Ben lay back in the water and held on to his kite. As the wind blew the kite, he was towed across the pond!

Ben decided to become a sailor when he grew up. His parents didn't want him to go to sea. In those days, not many children stayed in school for long. At the age of ten, Ben was taken out of school. His parents put him to work in the shop. Ben cut candlewicks and poured wax into candle molds.

Josiah hoped that one day Ben would take over the shop. But Ben hated candle-making. Two

years went by and nothing changed. Ben still hated the work. He wasn't going to follow in his father's footsteps.

His parents decided that Ben must become an apprentice. This was common for boys in colonial days.

CANDLE-MAKING

TALLOW (SOLID ANIMAL FAT FROM SHEEP AND CATTLE) OR WHALE OIL IS HEATED IN A COPPER VAT AND IMPURITIES ARE SKIMMED OFF.

THE HOT TALLOW IS POURED INTO MOLDS THAT ARE PREPARED WITH WICKS. THE MOLDS ARE THEN TRANSFERRED TO COLD WATER FOR HARDENING.

An apprentice had to work, without pay, for a skilled craftsman. In return, the craftsman taught the apprentice his trade. After about seven years, the

young man would be ready to earn money at the trade. But what trade should Ben learn?

Josiah took Ben to many different shops. They visited a furniture-maker and a bricklayer. They went to see a

brass-worker. They called on men who made pottery and silverware. Nothing appealed to Ben.

His mother and father had one more idea. Ben

had a brother, James, who was nine years older than he.

James was a printer. He already had an apprentice or two. However, James needed more help in his printing shop. Ben did not want to work for his brother. Still, it seemed better than laying bricks or making silverware. Besides, his father wasn't going to take "no" for an answer any longer.

So, in 1718, twelve-year-old Ben Franklin was apprenticed to his brother James. Papers were signed. He was to work for James for nine years, until he was twenty-one years old.

Chapter 3
Runaway

Ben left home and went to work in his brother's shop. James taught him to set type. Ben was a fast learner and was soon printing booklets and songs.

As the master, James had to pay for his apprentices' food and lodging. Ben moved in with a family. James's other apprentices lived there, too. James paid the family to provide Ben with meals and a bed.

Ben thought of a way to raise some cash. He proposed a deal. James should stop paying the family to feed Ben. Instead, James should

give Ben the meal money. Ben would feed himself—on just half the money James had been paying the family for his meals. Ben asked only one thing. Any meal money he didn't spend, he could keep. James agreed to the deal.

The young apprentice found a book on cooking with vegetables. He stopped eating meat. He lived on rice, boiled potatoes, and a cornmeal mush called hasty pudding. To his brother's surprise, Ben was able to save part of his meal money. He spent it on books.

Ben liked to read poetry. He decided to write a few poems of his own. In November 1718, the pirate known as Blackbeard was killed. Ben wrote a poem about it that began:

Will you hear of a bloody battle,
Lately fought upon the seas?
It will make your ears rattle,
And your admiration cease.

James printed Ben's poems. He sent Ben out into the streets to sell them. Ben's poem

about a drowning became very popular. It was called "The Lighthouse Tragedy." Soon the people of Boston were talking about the twelve-year-old poet.

Another of Ben's jobs was to help print the *Boston Gazette*. It was one of America's first newspapers. Then, in 1721, James began his own paper, the *New England Courant*. Ben printed the *Courant* and delivered copies to customers.

Ben enjoyed the work, but his brother was a harsh master. James wanted to show his other apprentices that he did not favor Ben. When Ben made mistakes, James beat him. Ben would then talk back. James would only beat him some more.

Around April Fools' Day of 1722, Ben decided to play a trick on his brother. He began writing funny articles about life in Boston. He didn't sign them with his own name. Instead, he made up a woman's name: Silence Dogood.

Late at night, Ben slipped the articles under the door of the print shop. James found them.

He liked Silence Dogood's articles so much that he printed them in the *Courant*. They appeared for half a year. People in Boston wondered: Who *was* Silence Dogood? Ben even heard James talking about Silence with his friends. Finally, in the fall of 1722, Ben revealed the truth. *He* was Silence Dogood.

Most readers laughed. But James was angry at being fooled.

Meanwhile, James Franklin was in trouble. He criticized the English officials who ran Massachusetts. His writings in the *Courant* landed him in jail for a month. That didn't stop James. In early 1723, an order was issued. James Franklin could no longer print the *New England Courant.*

James thought of a way to get around the order. He would list his seventeen-year-old brother Ben as the *Courant's* publisher! But secretly, James would still tell Ben what to do. What if James was asked how an apprentice could run the paper? He had an answer for that, too. James drew up papers saying that Ben had finished his apprenticeship and was now on his own. But James also made secret papers. These said that Ben must be his apprentice for four more years.

The scheme worked—for a while. The problem was, Ben wanted to really be publisher. He felt that he could run the paper, and he didn't like serving as his brother's puppet. The two of them fought more than ever. James's way to settle things was to beat Ben.

There came a day when James hit him once too often. Ben decided to run away. A runaway apprentice could be punished if he was caught,

AN APPRENTICE

SOME APPRENTICES STARTED AS YOUNG AS 7 OR 8

THEY WEREN'T PAID BUT LEARNED A TRADE

ABOUT 7 YEARS LATER, THE APPRENTICE WAS READY
TO GET A PAYING JOB

but Ben figured his brother wouldn't come after him. If James tried to catch him, Ben might reveal the scheme for running the newspaper. James could end up in jail again.

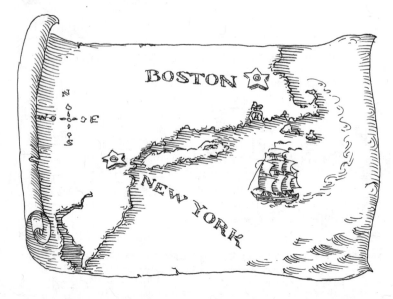

A friend of Ben's helped him stow away on a ship. In the fall of 1723, Ben boarded the ship with just a few coins in his pocket. Three days later he was in New York City, 200 miles from home.

Chapter 4
Ben Franklin, Printer

As Ben had expected, James did not try to track him down. Ben couldn't find printing work in New York, though. He went on to Philadelphia, Pennsylvania. The runaway apprentice made half the trip by boat. He walked the other fifty miles.

Ben arrived in Philadelphia tired and dirty. His extra shirts and stockings were bulging out of his pockets. He was hungry, so he bought three penny rolls at a bakery.

Ben stuck two of the rolls under his arms. He stuffed the third into his mouth. As Ben walked along, a girl named Deborah Read saw him from her doorway. She burst out laughing at the sight.

Ben rented a room from Debby's family. He found a job with a printer. Ben did so well that he was soon running the business.

The governor of Pennsylvania saw Ben's printing work. He was impressed. The governor offered to help set Ben up in business. If Ben would visit England to buy printing supplies, the governor promised, he would pay the bills.

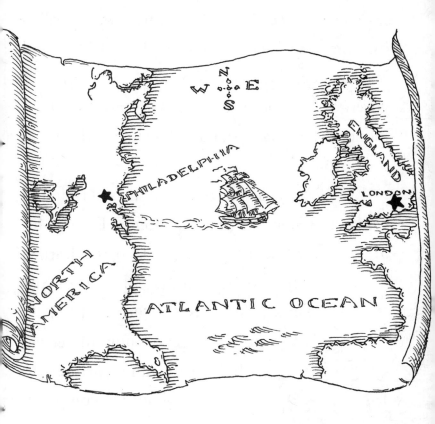

LONDON

The eighteen-year-old printer was thrilled by the offer. He sailed in late 1724, and reached London on Christmas Eve. But the governor had been all talk. He never sent the money. Ben was stranded in England, 3,000 miles from home.

But Ben made the best of things. He found work at a London printing house. During his year and a half in England, he learned more about printing. He also met famous scientists and authors. In 1725, at the age of only nineteen, he wrote and printed a booklet about religion.

For fun, he swam in the Thames River. Once he swam more than three miles on a bet. As crowds watched him swim, Ben had an idea. He would stay in England to run a swimming school. 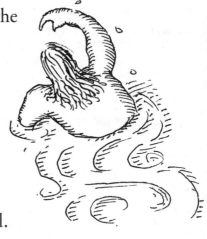 Fortunately for America, he changed his mind.

In the fall of 1726, Ben returned to Philadelphia. For a while he worked for a printer. Then in 1728 he went into the printing business for himself. The next year, he began to publish his own newspaper. It was called the *Pennsylvania Gazette*. Ben was its editor, printer, and star reporter. He drew one of the first cartoons to appear in an American newspaper. His paper was also one of the first to print a map with an article.

PRINTING IN COLONIAL TIMES

THE COMPOSER LAYS THE TYPE OUT ON A COMPOSING STICK, THEN PLACES IT IN A FRAME CALLED A GALLEY. THE GALLEYS ARE GIVEN TO THE STONEMAN, WHO COMBINES THEM TIGHTLY TOGETHER ON A FORM.
THE FORM IS GIVEN TO THE PRESSMEN, WHO SET IT ON THE STONE. THEN INK IS BEATEN ONTO THE TYPE WITH MALLETS.
WET PAPER IS PLACED ON THE TYMPAN, SECURED BY

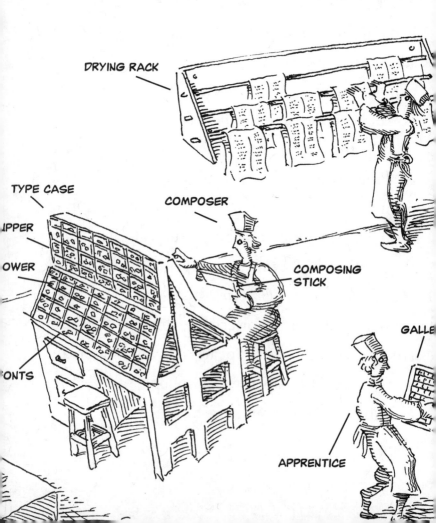

DRYING RACK

TYPE CASE

IPPER

OWER

ONTS

COMPOSER

COMPOSING STICK

GALLE

APPRENTICE

THE FRISKET, AND FOLDED OVER THE INKED TYPE.
THE STONE IS THEN ROLLED UNDER THE PLATEN, WHERE
A PRESSMAN PULLS DOWN THE LEVER AND THE TYPE IS
PRESSED ONTO THE PAPER.

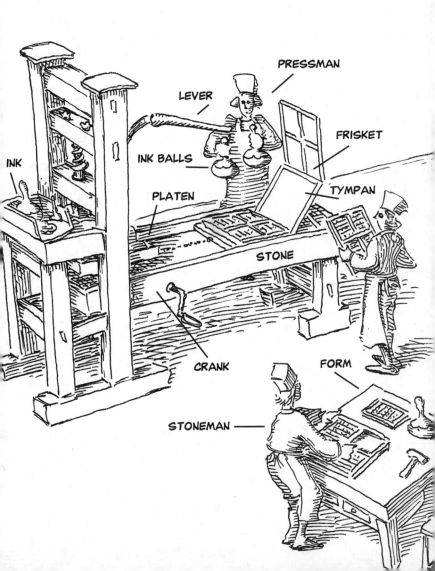

Besides news, his paper offered jokes and riddles. When there was little to report, Ben invented "news items." For example, he ran a

story about a man who happened to be in a canoe with his wife and his fiddle. The canoe overturned. The wife could not swim. But the man, Franklin reported, saved his fiddle "and let his wife go to the bottom." If there were not enough letters to the e d i t o r, F r a n k l i n made up let-

ters. He signed them with fake names. He also spiced up his paper with advice to the lovelorn.

His own love life was bumpy. During the time he had lived with the Reads, Ben had fallen in love with Debby. She was the girl who thought he looked so funny when he first came to Philadelphia. After Ben returned from England, he and Debby wanted to marry. But they each had a problem.

Ben had a child with another woman. Who was she? To this day, we do not know. The baby was born in 1730 or 1731 and was named William Franklin. Ben arranged to raise the boy.

Debby had married another man while Ben was away. The man left Debby. It was believed that he died in a barroom fight.

This was not known for sure, however. Under the law, if her husband was alive, Debby must not remarry. If she did, she could be jailed.

Debby and Ben found a solution. On September 1, 1730, they had a common-law wedding. This meant that they would live as husband and wife without a legal ceremony. Debby would also treat William as her son.

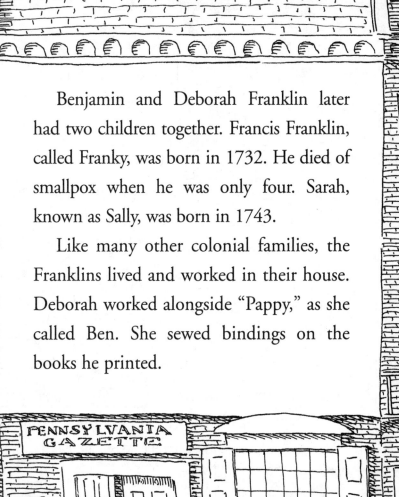

Benjamin and Deborah Franklin later had two children together. Francis Franklin, called Franky, was born in 1732. He died of smallpox when he was only four. Sarah, known as Sally, was born in 1743.

Like many other colonial families, the Franklins lived and worked in their house. Deborah worked alongside "Pappy," as she called Ben. She sewed bindings on the books he printed.

PENNSYLVANIA GAZETTE

With Debby's help, Ben became the largest bookseller in the colonies. *The Pennsylvania Gazette* became the leading newspaper.

In those times, almanacs were very popular. These booklets gave weather forecasts and other information for the coming year. Ben printed almanacs written

by other people. Then, in 1732, he decided to create his own almanac. He pretended that the author was named Richard Saunders. Richard was supposed to be a poor but lovable man. *Poor Richard's Almanac* was first issued for 1733. Franklin continued it every year until 1758.

Poor Richard's Almanac became the most popular almanac in America. It sold 10,000 copies a year. There were two reasons for its success. First, each year Poor Richard told a little about his life. Reading it was like following a soap opera today.

Poor Richard's sayings were the other big attraction. The first almanac introduced the saying: "Great talkers, little doers." Sayings

for 1750 included: "Little strokes fell great oaks."
In 1753 Poor Richard warned: "Haste makes
waste." Many of Poor Richard's sayings are still
popular today.

Actually, Poor Richard—or rather Ben
Franklin—did not make up most of the sayings.
Often he just improved old sayings. For example,
there was a saying: "Help thyself and God will
help thee." Ben changed it to "God helps them
that help themselves."

People began to quote Poor Richard's sayings. A child given a penny might be told, "A penny saved is a penny earned." At bedtime, children were reminded, "Early to bed and early to rise, makes a man healthy, wealthy, and wise."

Poor Richard made Ben wealthy. In fact, he was rich enough to stop working as a printer. In 1748, he placed his printing business in the hands of a partner.

He didn't retire, though. Ben was just forty-two years old. There was so much he hoped to do. He felt like he was just starting out in life.

Chapter 5
Doing Good

"What is serving God?" Poor Richard asked in 1747. His answer: "Doing good to Man." After retiring from printing, Ben Franklin tried to do just that.

He had always liked science. Electricity fascinated him. Besides doing his kite experiment, Ben made an early electric battery. In fact, he coined the terms electric battery, electric shock, and conductor.

EARLY BATTERY–MAKING

ELECTROSTATIC MACHINE

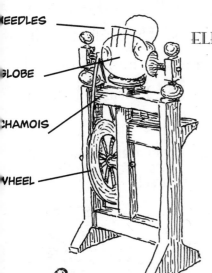

NEEDLES

GLOBE

CHAMOIS

WHEEL

A REVOLVING GLASS GLOBE RUBS A PIECE OF SOFT LEATHER CALLED A CHAMOIS TO PRODUCE STATIC ELETRICITY. SEWING NEEDLES TRANSFER THE ELECTRIC CHARGE FROM THE GLOBE TO THE LEYDEN JARS.

THE CHARGE IS CARRIED DOWN INTO THE JAR THROUGH A ROD AND WIRES TO THE WATER AND METAL FOIL INSIDE. THIS CAUSES AN OPPOSITE CHARGE TO FORM ON A BAND OF METAL FOIL ON THE OUTSIDE OF THE JAR.

LEYDEN JAR

MULTIPLE LEYDEN JARS ARE CONNECTED TO PRODUCE THIS 18TH–CENTURY ELECTRICAL CHARGE STORAGE DEVICE.

Ben once tried to cook a turkey using electricity from Leyden jars. Unfortunately he touched the wires and knocked himself out. "I wanted to cook a turkey but I nearly killed a goose," he joked. Still, he believed that one day people would cook and do other daily tasks with electricity. He was right, of course!

On his voyages, Franklin became the first scientist to study a powerful ocean current. He named it the Gulf Stream. Ben found that it could slow down or speed up ships. The Gulf Stream was warmer than the water around it,

Franklin learned. To find the Gulf Stream, sailors just had to dip a thermometer into the ocean.

Franklin did a clever experiment with heat. He got many cloth patches from a tailor. They were different colors—black, blue, green, purple, red, yellow, and white. On a sunny winter morning he laid the patches on the snow. After a while, he saw that the black

patch had sunk the deepest into the snow. The white patch had sunk the least. Why?

Dark colors take in more heat from the sun than light ones. Therefore the black cloth had melted more snow than any of the other colored cloths. To this day, people take Franklin's advice. On hot, sunny days they wear light colors to stay cool.

Ben's ideas about health were very modern. At the time, people thought that strange

vapors in the air caused illness. Although germs weren't yet known, Franklin said that many diseases were spread from person to person. Fresh air was healthy, he argued. People should sleep with an open window. And they should take a daily "air bath." This meant sitting naked with the windows open—as Ben did for an hour each day. He also told people to exercise. Besides swimming and walking, he lifted dumbbells until he was in his eighties.

Everything interested Ben Franklin. One day, Ben and his son Billy were riding through Maryland. Suddenly a tornado appeared. "It was in the form of a sugar loaf, spinning on its point, moving up the hill towards us," he wrote. What did Ben do? He rode his horse toward the twister! Billy followed.

They kept pace with the tornado for nearly a mile. They only stopped when tree branches flew near them. It was a dangerous thing to do, but Ben was curious.

"What good is science that does not apply to some use?" Ben once asked. He invented a number of things to improve people's lives. The lightning rod is the best known. The Franklin stove was another of his creations. Ben invented this heating device around 1740. Franklin stoves directed heat from a fireplace into a room instead of letting most of it go up the chimney. They were placed in many homes.

FRANKLIN STOVE

THE FRANKLIN STOVE IS AN
IRON BOX THAT FITS
INSIDE THE FIREPLACE.
IT IS MORE HEAT- AND
FUEL-EFFICIENT THAN AN
OPEN HEARTH.

AIR IS HEATED AS IT FLOWS
THROUGH THE CHAMBERS OF
THE BOX, AND THEN EXITS
FROM THE SIDE PANELS.

CUTAWAY

AIRBOX

The oil street lamps of the time often burned out quickly. Ben decided to design better lamps. He invented a lamp with a squarish shape. It had a funnel at the top to draw up the smoke. Franklin lamps burned all night.

Ben's eyes weakened with age. The time came when he needed two pairs of eyeglasses. One pair was for reading. The second was for

seeing things far away. Keeping track of two pairs of glasses was a bother. In 1784 he invented bifocals. Lenses for both close and distant vision were combined into one pair of glasses. Millions of people wear bifocals today.

TOP FOR DISTANCE

BOTTOM FOR READING

Franklin loved music. He wrote songs. He played the violin, guitar, and harp. Around 1761, Ben invented a new instrument. Different-sized glass bowls were kept spinning on a cradle. The bowls'

GLASS HARMONICA

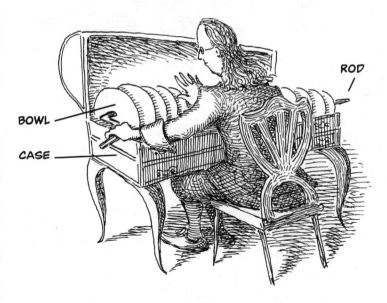

ROD

BOWL

CASE

rims were wet. When a person held his fingers against the wet spinning bowls, it made music. Franklin's new instrument was called the glass harmonica. It was played at concerts in Europe and America for about forty years.

Another of Ben's inventions was an artificial arm. He used it to take books down from high shelves. The device was later used for taking items off top shelves in grocery stores.

His inventions could have made him a fortune, but Ben refused to profit from them. "The opportunity to serve others" was payment enough for him, he explained.

Philadelphia was more than just a place to live for Ben. He loved the city. He wanted to improve it in any way he could. That led him into public service.

Books were costly and hard to find in colonial days. In 1731, Ben founded the Library Company of Philadelphia. The members paid dues. The money was spent on books, which the members could borrow for free. This was a step in creating America's public library system.

Fire was a great danger in an age when houses were mostly made of wood. Ben

EARLY METHODS
AND EQUIPMENT
FOR FIREFIGHTING

A "BUCKET BRIGADE": LINE FROM THE WATER SOURCE TO THE FIRE

B "PUMPER": AN EARLY VERSION OF THE FIRE ENGINE

C BASKET DEVICE FOR LOWERING TRAPPED VICTIMS

D SACKS FOR REMOVING PERSONAL BELONGINGS

founded the Union Fire Company in 1736. It was America's first volunteer fire department. Philadelphia became one of the world's most fire-safe cities.

Not even Ben Franklin dreamed of a day when there would be telephones, TVs, and computers. The colonists stayed in touch by mail. But mail often came late or not at all.

Franklin became Philadelphia's postmaster in 1737. English officials noted his fine work. They named him acting postmaster for America in 1753. Ben hired more letter carriers. He made better mail routes. Mail delivery in the colonies was greatly improved.

PHILADELPHIA ACADEMY

Philadelphia needed a hospital and a school for higher learning. Again, Ben stepped forward. He helped found the Philadelphia Academy. Later it became the University of Pennsylvania. The same year the Academy opened—1751—he helped start the Pennsylvania Hospital. It was the country's first general hospital. By the 1750s, Philadelphia was America's leading city. Much of the credit belonged to Benjamin Franklin.

Franklin entered politics in 1736. He was chosen clerk of Pennsylvania's Assembly, or legislature, which met in Philadelphia. For fifteen years he recorded debates and votes. But, he later recalled, "I grew at length tired with sitting there to hear the debates, in which, as clerk, I could take no part." He didn't want to just write about events. He wanted to take part in them. In 1751 he ran for an Assembly seat and won.

Three years later, the French and Indian War (1754–1763) began. This war was fought over control of North America. On one side was France, helped by her Indian allies. On the other was England, aided by her thirteen American Colonies. Ben raised troops to help England. He even served as a general. With his son William's help, Ben led troops to

WILLIAM PENN

the frontier. The father and son built forts. They organized patrols to protect settlers. More trouble was brewing. Pennsylvania had been named for the Penns. They were an English family who had founded the colony. The Penns still ran Pennsylvania, but during the French and Indian War, the colonists became angry at the Penns. They claimed that the family wasn't

RICHARD PENN

paying enough to fight the war. In 1757, the Pennsylvania Assembly asked Franklin to visit England. His job was to get money from the Penns.

Debby stayed home with thirteen-year-old Sally. William went along with his father. Their ship was almost captured by French ships. Off England, they were nearly ship-wrecked. But they made it through the fog and arrived in London in July.

Ben had no idea at the time that he would spend most of his remaining years overseas.

Chapter 6
Revolution

The Franklins moved into a London apartment. Ben showed Billy places he had known in his days as a young printer. Besides helping

his father, Billy studied law in London. He became friends with rich young English

people. Soon Billy seemed more English than American. Ben was pleased. England ruled the colonies. Ben hoped that one day Billy would serve in the English government.

Ben needed three years to complete his mission. In 1760, the British government agreed that Pennsylvania deserved help. The Penns had to pay more money for the French and Indian War. But the Franklins did not go home yet. Ben enjoyed the attention he was getting as America's greatest scientist and inventor. Billy was about to get an important job.

In August 1762, the king of England

named William Franklin royal governor of New
Jersey. Soon after being
named to run New Jersey for
the king, William was married. His wife was named
Elizabeth Downes; he had
met her at a party. The newly-
weds sailed to America. They
settled in Burlington, New
Jersey. Ben returned to his wife
and daughter. Only fifteen
miles separated Philadelphia

KING GEORGE III

and Burlington. Ben and his son saw each
other often.

WILLIAM FRANKLIN
GOVERNOR OF NEW JERSEY

For two years, Ben spent a lot of time on post-office business. But there was new trouble with the Penns. The colonists wanted Pennsylvania to be taken away from the Penns.

They wanted their colony placed under the king's direct rule. In late 1764, Benjamin was sent back to England to make this happen.

He had been in England for a few weeks when a more serious problem arose. England had won the French and Indian War, but the war had been costly. England needed money. To help raise funds, England passed the Stamp Act in early 1765. The new law taxed Americans on newspapers and other paper goods.

THE STAMP ACT

STAMP

TO HELP PAY ITS DEBTS, THE BRITISH GOVERNMENT CREATED A TAX IN THE FORM OF A STAMP. THIS TAX STAMP WAS REQUIRED ON ALL PUBLICATIONS AND LEGAL PAPERS THROUGHOUT THE COLONIES.

English people asked the famous American his opinion about the new tax. Franklin opposed it, but not very strongly. He didn't know that, 3,000 miles away, Americans were enraged by the tax. In fact, the colonists were rioting. When Philadelphians learned that Franklin wasn't fighting the tax with all his might, a mob threatened to burn his home. William Franklin rushed from New Jersey to take Sally away. Deborah refused to budge. She prepared to defend her home with a gun. Luckily, the rioters stayed away.

Ben learned about events at home. He saw that Americans wanted him to speak for them. He decided to express their anger—even if he didn't yet feel it deeply.

Almost overnight, he became a leading Stamp Act foe. He wrote to British newspapers. He debated with British lawmakers. And, in early 1766, he argued against the Stamp Act before Parliament—Britain's lawmaking body.

BOSTON TEA PARTY

DECEMBER 16, 1773

TO PROTEST THE TAX ON TEA, PATRIOTS DISGUISED AS INDIANS BOARDED THREE BRITISH SHIPS AND DUMPED TONS OF TEA INTO BOSTON HARBOR.

A few days later, the tax was repealed. Americans gave Franklin much of the credit.

However, there was talk of new English taxes. Ben felt that he couldn't go home during this crisis. Also, other colonies besides Pennsylvania were asking him to handle their problems with England.

Britain *did* pass more taxes—on tea and other items. As Britain taxed the Americans and sent in soldiers to enforce its laws, Franklin changed. No longer did he just *act* as America's spokesman. He truly hated England. He spoke so angrily that the English called him the "prime conductor" of the American rebels.

On Christmas Eve of 1774, William wrote to his father with bad news. Deborah Franklin, Ben's wife of forty-four years, had died of a stroke. William blamed Ben for her death. He felt that her heart had been broken because Ben had been away

for ten years. Ben knew that there was some truth
to this, but it hurt to hear it from Billy. He also
knew that he and his son were growing apart.
Ben was fighting for America's rights. Billy was
the king's governor in New Jersey. He sided
with England.

Ben was at a low point in his life. His wife
was dead. His son was angry at him. They were
on different sides of a giant political fight.
England blamed him for the trouble with
America. Ben decided that he belonged back in

his own country with his family. In March of 1775, he sailed for home. On April 19—while he was at sea—war broke out between England and America.

Chapter 7
Creating a New Nation

Ben reached Philadelphia on May 5, 1775. The very next morning he was asked to serve in the Continental Congress. This was a meeting of American leaders. It opened in Philadelphia on May 10. Its main job was to win the war against England.

At age sixty-nine, Franklin worked twelve-hour days in Congress. One of his jobs was to organize the United States Postal Service. He soon had mail moving swiftly among all thirteen colonies. This was crucial. To win the war, people throughout America had to work together.

Another job didn't go as well. In the spring of 1776, Ben was sent north to Canada with three other men. They tried to convince the Canadians to fight on America's side. Their efforts failed. Worse still, Ben nearly died from the cold and the strain of the trip. But he made it back to Philadelphia in time to take part in the great question of the day.

CONTINENTAL SOLDIER

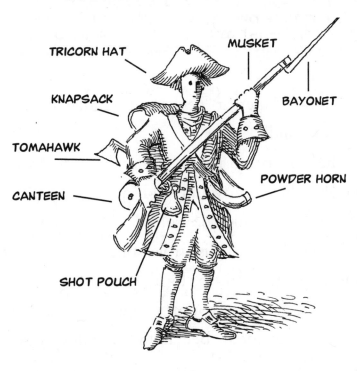

TRICORN HAT

MUSKET

KNAPSACK

BAYONET

TOMAHAWK

CANTEEN

POWDER HORN

SHOT POUCH

EARLY FLAGS

WHEN THE THIRTEEN COLONIES WENT TO WAR AGAINST ENGLAND, THE AMERICAN COLONISTS WANTED THEIR OWN FLAG TO REPRESENT THE LAND THEY WERE FIGHTING FOR. HERE ARE SOME OF THE FLAGS COLONISTS USED DURING THE REVOLUTION.

Should America declare its independence from England?

The American people were divided. Many thought the war would end quickly and the tax trouble would be solved. Then America could return to English rule. But just as many Americans wanted to break free of England and form a new country. America's leaders were also divided. Benjamin Franklin was a leader of the congressmen who wanted to create a new nation.

Congress was to vote on the issue in July of 1776. If the vote came out for independence, America would need to explain exactly why it was breaking away from England. Congress asked five men to write a Declaration of Independence. Benjamin Franklin was one. Thomas Jefferson of Virginia was another.

THOMAS JEFFERSON

Jefferson did most of the writing. Ben made a few changes. For example, Jefferson wrote: "We hold these truths to be sacred and undeniable." Ben improved it to: "We hold these truths to be self-evident." This was a simpler way to say that some things were plain to see.

Congress voted on July 2. With a little arm-twisting by Ben, the vote came out strongly for independence. The thirteen Colonies were now the United States of America. Congress approved the Declaration two days later. Ever since, Americans have honored that day—July 4, 1776—as the country's birthday.

At the signing of the Declaration, Ben reportedly made a famous comment. John Hancock was president of Congress. He wanted everyone to cooperate. "We must all hang together," he said.

"Yes," answered Ben. "We must all hang together, or most assuredly we shall all hang separately!" He meant that they must work together—or else! If America lost the war, England might hang each leader by the neck.

Ben was happy about independence, but his heart was heavy for personal reasons. Many families, including the Franklins, were split by the war. Ben begged his son to quit as New Jersey governor. He wanted William to side with America. The father and son wrote letters back and forth. They had some heart-to heart talks. Ben could not convince William to leave his post. He had become an English gentleman—just as Benjamin had wanted.

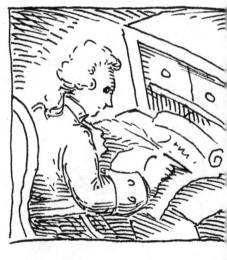

One by one, England's colonial

governors were removed from office. They were replaced with Americans. William was thrown out of office. He was put in jail in a filthy cell where

he nearly died. Still, William Franklin stayed loyal to England.

"Nothing ever hurt me so much," Ben said about his son siding with Britain. A word from Ben to Congress might have freed William. But Ben never spoke up for his son. The United States was fighting for its life. He felt that special treatment for William would be unfair.

In Britain, people were more afraid of Benjamin Franklin than of George Washington and his army. Rumors spread that Benjamin was a wizard. He had invented weapons that could destroy all of England! He had a tiny device that could turn buildings to ash! He had reflecting mirrors that would burn the British navy! He had an "electrical machine" that would flip England upside down like a pancake!

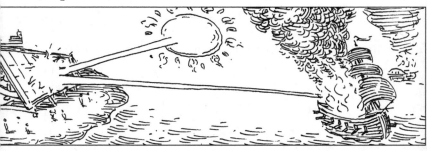

Of course, Ben had no such weapons, and for quite some time it looked like America would lose the war. Then, in the fall of 1776, Congress sent Franklin overseas on a mission that could decide the war. He was to convince France to help America fight England.

Once in France, Franklin found that British spies were everywhere. He couldn't always meet with French leaders. Sometimes messages had to be written in invisible ink and signed with secret code names. But, after a year of work, Ben got what he came for.

France joined the American side in early 1778. Alone, the young United States might not have beaten England. Things changed after France stepped in. French money, troops, ships, and

weapons helped the United States win its war for independence in 1783. Franklin signed the peace treaty made that year.

Ben wanted to go home after the war was won, but Congress asked him to stay in France. There, he would be a spokesman for the new country. Finally, in 1785, Congress said that he could leave. That summer, he went to Southampton, England, to sail for home.

William Franklin had been set free during the war. He had fled to England. William learned that his father was in Southampton. Benjamin was seventy-nine years old. William was fifty-four. The father and son who had flown the kite in the storm saw each other one last time. Billy tried to make up, but his father refused to forgive him for having sided with England.

Ben arrived back in Philadelphia in September of 1785. Ahead of him was a quiet retirement—or so he thought.

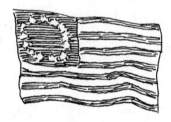

PENNSYLVANIA STATEHOUSE–INDEPENDENCE HALL

THE LIBERTY BELL WAS CAST

IN LONDON IN 1751 TO CELEBRATE PENNSYLVANIA'S ORIGINAL 1701 CONSTITUTION. THE BELL CRACKED SOON AFTER, BUT WAS RECAST AND HUNG IN THE PENNSYLVANIA STATEHOUSE, WHERE IT RANG ON IMPORTANT OCCASIONS. (IT RANG ON JULY 8, 1776 AFTER THE FIRST PUBLIC READING OF THE DECLARATION OF INDEPENDENCE.)

IT LATER DEVELOPED ANOTHER CRACK AND WAS LAST RUNG IN 1846.

INSCRIPTION:
"PROCLAIM LIBERTY THROUGHOUT ALL THE LAND UNTO ALL THE INHABITANTS THEREOF."

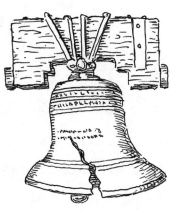

Chapter 8
A Rising Sun

Ben returned home a hero. He landed at the spot where he had entered Philadelphia as a teenaged runaway.

This time, cannons saluted him. Bells were rung. Speeches were made honoring the man who had done so much to win America's freedom. A few weeks later, he was elected governor of Pennsylvania.

The new nation was in trouble. The government was weak. There was no national currency. The army was tiny. If something wasn't done, the country might not last for long.

Something *was* done. A convention was held to make the government stronger. States chose leading men to attend. Ben Franklin of Pennsylvania was one of the delegates. The convention opened in Philadelphia in May 1787. Its members hammered out a

new framework of government: the U.S. Constitution.

At eighty-one, Franklin was the oldest delegate. When there were arguments, Ben told funny stories to calm things down. He also helped solve a big problem. The large states wanted to have the most say in the government. The small states feared that they wouldn't have much power. Franklin helped work out a solution. In the House of Representatives, large states would have more members than small states. But in the Senate, each state, regardless of size, would have two members.

Ben Franklin and the other Founding Fathers

signed the Constitution on September 17, 1787. As they did so, Ben pointed to the chair in which George Washington had sat. On the chair was a picture of the sun. During the convention, Ben had wondered whether it was supposed to be rising or setting. He was now so hopeful about the country that he knew. "It is a rising sun!" he exclaimed.

During his last years, Ben lived with his daughter Sally and her seven children. He served as the governor of Pennsylvania until 1788. That year, he was eighty-two years old. But by his own special way of counting he was only fifty-eight. After age seventy, Ben had

decided not to get any older. So, from then on, with each birthday he counted a year backwards!

One of Ben's final projects was to try to end slavery. He served as president of an anti-slavery society. His very last public act was to sign a paper that was sent to Congress. The paper asked that slavery be stopped.

Poor health made Ben spend much of his last two years in bed. He passed the time by listening to his grandchildren reciting their lessons. In the spring of 1790, he became very ill. Sally told him that he would live many more years. "I hope not," answered her father. He died a few hours later on April 17, 1790, at the age of eighty-four.

Tributes came in from around the world. Statues of him were built. Poems, articles, and

books were written about him. A saying from France became popular: "He snatched the lightning from the sky and the scepter from tyrants."

Ben Franklin deserved all the praise. He did so much in his long life. His greatest accomplishment is still going strong—the United States, the country that he helped create.

B Franklin

Timeline of Ben's Life

1706 —— Ben is born, January 17, in Boston, Massachusetts

1718 —— Ben is apprenticed to his brother, James

1722 —— Ben starts writing articles using the name "Silence Dogood"

1723 —— Ben runs away and ends up in Philadelphia, where he meets Debby

1724 —— Ben sails to England

1726 —— Ben returns to Philadelphia

1730 —— Ben and Debby get married
Ben's son, William, is born

1732 —— Ben publishes *Poor Richard's Almanac*

1752 —— Ben discovers the electrical nature of lightning, invents the lightning rod

1753 —— Ben is named postmaster for America

1766 —— Ben argues against the Stamp Act before Parliament

1774 —— Ben's wife, Debby, dies

1776 —— Ben helps write the Declaration of Independence

1783 —— Ben signs the peace treaty made between England and the United States

1785 —— Ben is elected governor of Pennsylvania

1787 —— Ben helps write the United States Constitution

1790 —— Ben dies on April 17, at the age of 84

Timeline of The World

Great Britain comes into being with the union of England and Scotland	1707
William Penn, founder of the colony of Pennsylvania, dies	1718
The Great Northern War between Sweden and Russia ends	1721
The first mercury thermometer is invented	1724
Peter the Great, king of Russia, dies	1725
Gulliver's Travels, by Jonathan Swift, is published	1726
The cuckoo clock is invented Opticians begin anchoring eyeglasses to the ears with side pieces called temples	1730
George Washington, the first U.S. president, is born	1732
Chinese invade and conquer Tibet	1752
The historic Liberty Bell is hung at Independence Hall in Philadelphia	1753
The French and Indian War begins in America	1754
Hydrogen is discovered The first paved sidewalk is laid in London	1766
Louis XVI becomes king of France	1774
The American Revolution begins The city of San Francisco is founded	1775
The first parachute is demonstrated	1783
Jacob Ludwig Grimm, the German writer of Grimm's Fairy tales, is born	1785
The first steamboat is built	1787
The French Revolution begins	1790